SHAKESPEARE'S

JULIUS CAESAR

RETOLD BY
CARL BOWEN

ILLUSTRATED BY
EDUARDO GARCIA

raintree

a Capstone company — publishers for children

D1081025

www.raintreepublishers.co.uk
Visit our website to find out
more information about
Raintree books.

To order:
☎ Phone 0845 6044371
🖷 Fax +44 (0) 1865 312263
✉ Email myorders@raintreepublishers.co.uk

Customers from outside the UK please telephone +44 1865 312262

Raintree is an imprint of Capstone Global Library Limited, a company incorporated in
England and Wales having its registered office at 7 Pilgrim Street, London, EC4V 6LB –
Registered company number: 6695582

Art Director: Kay Fraser
Graphic Designer: Hilary Wacholz
Editor: Diyan Leake
Production Specialist: Victoria Fitzgerald
Originated by Capstone Global Library Ltd
Printed in China

ISBN 978 1 406 24327 7
17 16
10 9 8 7 6 5 4 3

British Library Cataloguing in Publication Data
A full catalogue record for this book is available from the British Library.

CONTENTS

SHAKESPEARE

WILLIAM SHAKESPEARE WAS ONE OF
THE GREATEST WRITERS THE WORLD
HAS EVER KNOWN.

HE WROTE COMEDIES, TRAGEDIES,
HISTORIES, AND ROMANCES ABOUT
ANCIENT HEROES, BRUTAL WARS, AND
MAGICAL CREATURES.

THIS IS ONE OF THOSE STORIES . . .

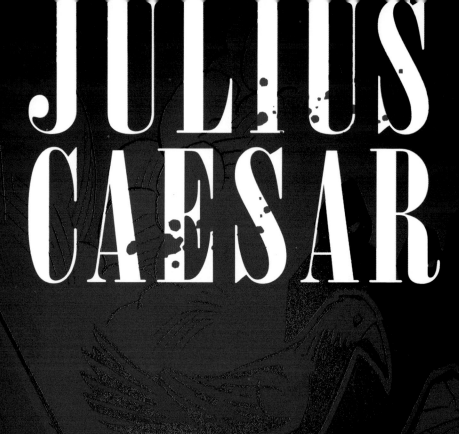

JULIUS CAESAR

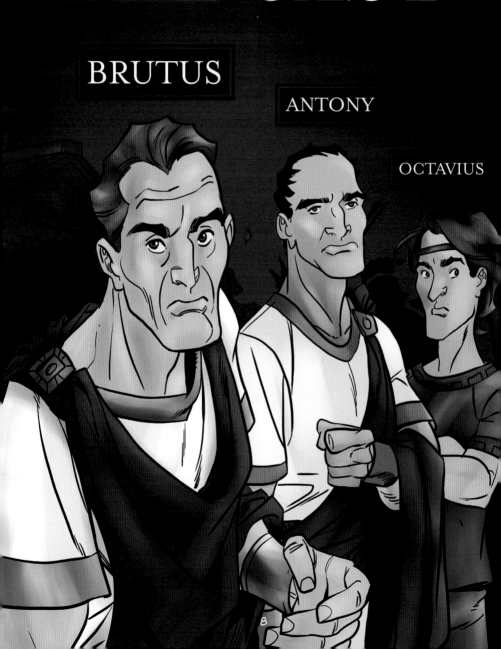

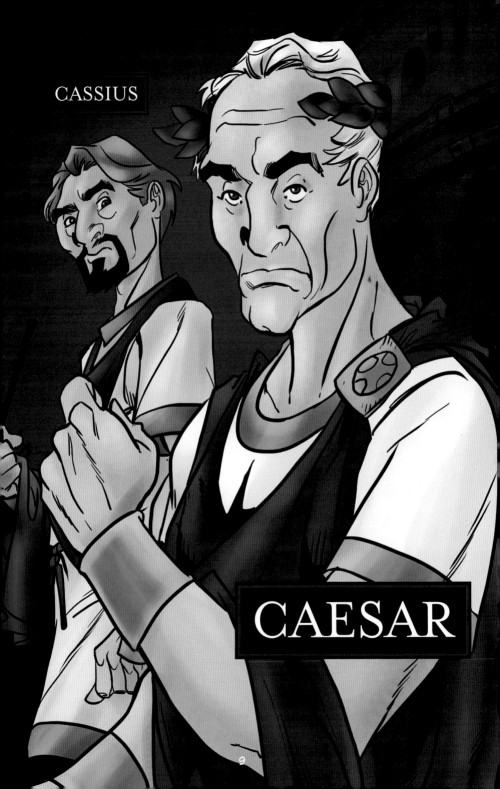

CASSIUS

CAESAR

PROLOGUE

Julius Caesar was one of the most powerful men in Rome.

He led his armies to countless victories.

His chief rival for power was Pompey, a well-loved Roman politician.

Pompey's friends in the senate did everything he asked them to do.

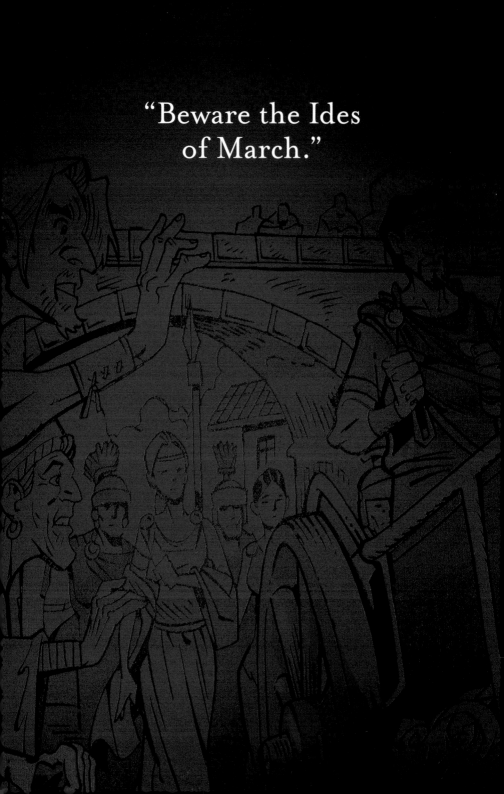

ACT ONE

Rome, 48 BC. Romans flocked to the streets to celebrate the end of their civil war.

Get to work, you lazy creatures! Is this a holiday?

You there! What is your trade?

Why, sir, I am a carpenter.

Why are you not in your shop today?!

We are celebrating Caesar's victorious return!

You are worse than senseless!

Do you also celebrate Pompey's death?

Oh, you cruel men of Rome! Be gone!

Vanish, tongue-tied, in your guilt!

Allow no images to be hung with Caesar's symbols.

RRRIIP!!

Later that day, Caesar and his followers entered the city arena.

Most celebrated his return . . .

. . . but not all.

Caesar, hear me!

Beware the Ides of March!

Caesar ignored the soothsayer.

As Brutus and Cassius spoke, they heard three cheers from the arena.

HAIL CAESAR!!!

HAIL CAESAR!!!

HAIL CAESAR!!!

With each cheer, they feared that Caesar had been crowned.

As Caesar passed by . . .

That Cassius has a lean and hungry look to him.

Such men are dangerous.

Casca, tell us, what is the news from the arena?

A crown was offered to Caesar.

Was the crown offered to him three times?

Yes, and he refused it three times.

Who offered him the crown?

Mark Antony did.

Please come to my home tomorrow and speak with me, Cassius.

I will do so, Brutus.

You are indeed noble, Brutus. Yet, I see your allegiance can be changed.

Let Caesar seat himself upon the throne!

For **we** will shake him off, or all will suffer worse days.

CRACKKK

Casca, returning home from Caesar's palace, was caught out in the storm.

Cassius! What a night this is!

A very pleasant night to honest men, Casca.

It is the role of men to fear and tremble when the gods send storms like this one.

I know a man far worse than this dreadful night.

'Tis Caesar that you speak of.

By my dagger, I will end Caesar's reign.

Cassius told Casca of his plan to kill Julius Caesar.

What say you, Casca?

I will go as far as you do, Cassius.

There's a bargain made.

"Cowards die many times before their deaths. The valiant never taste of death but once."

ACT
TWO

Should Rome be ruled by one man?

Since Cassius first spoke to me against Caesar, I have not slept.

The time spent waiting to act on a dreadful deed is like a nightmare.

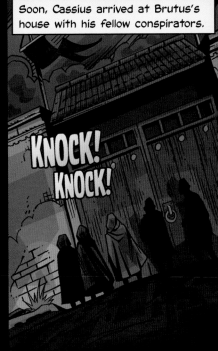

Soon, Cassius arrived at Brutus's house with his fellow conspirators.

KNOCK! KNOCK!

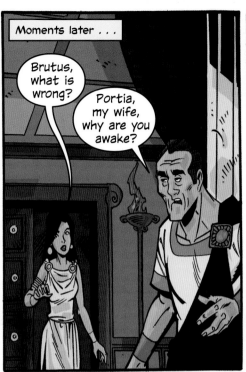

Moments later . . .

Brutus, what is wrong?

Portia, my wife, why are you awake?

My dear lord, share with me your cause of grief.

Oh, the gods gave me a loving wife.

In time, you shall hear the secrets of my heart . . .

Later, in Caesar's palace . . .

Help, help! They killed Caesar!

. . . Caesar's wife was having a terrible nightmare.

When she awoke, she realized it was 15 March — the Ides of March.

Oh! Today is the day the soothsayer warned Caesar about!

You should not leave our house today, Caesar.

A man cannot hide from the fate of the gods. I will go forth.

33

But the senators have concluded this day to give the crown to you, mighty Caesar.

If you send them word that you will not come today, they might change their minds . . .

How foolish do your fears seem now? I am ashamed that I listened to you.

Brutus, why are you here so early? What is the time?

Caesar, it is eight o'clock.

Just then, Mark Antony arrived.

Antony arrives as well!

Good morrow, Antony.

To you as well, most noble Caesar.

All of my good friends are here with me today!

Each of you must come and share some of my wine!

We will, Caesar.

But soon, you will wish your *friends* had been far away . . .

And after, like friends, we will leave together.

Oh, poor Caesar . . .

ACT THREE

Caesar led his followers to the Capitol, where it was certain he would be named King of Rome.

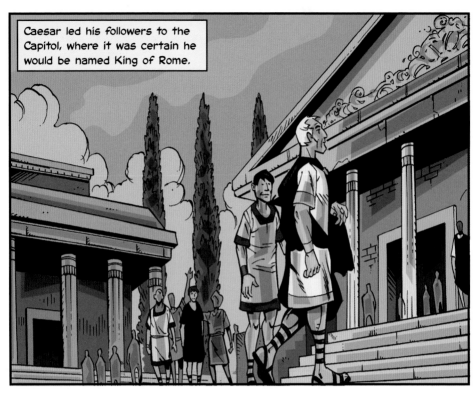

On the way inside, Caesar stopped to mock the soothsayer.

The Ides of March have come, yet I still live.

Aye, Caesar . . .

. . . but the day is not yet over.

The senators were waiting for Caesar. As Caesar spoke with them, the conspirators whispered amongst themselves . . .

Trebonius leads Mark Antony away. Now is the time . . .

Where is Metellus? Let him go ask his favour of Caesar.

Metellus, a conspirator, had a brother who had been banished.

Please, Caesar. Allow my brother to return home.

No. By law, I cannot.

But, sir, please –

Do not beg me, or I will strike you like a dog.

Is there no voice more worthy than my own to beg Caesar on my behalf?

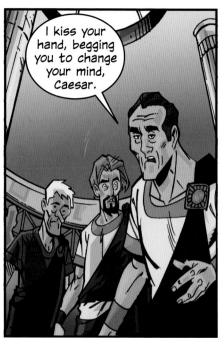

I kiss your hand, begging you to change your mind, Caesar.

Pardon, Caesar. I, Cassius, beg for Metellus's brother, too.

I am constant as the northern star.

Metellus's brother must stay banished.

For liberty! For Rome!

Tyranny is dead!

Kneel, Romans, and let us wash our hands in Caesar's blood.

Then we shall walk to the marketplace and cry "Peace! Freedom! And Liberty!"

When Antony returned . . .

Oh, mighty Caesar!

Later, the citizens gathered at the senate for Caesar's funeral.

Caesar's killers arrived first to explain what they had done.

Caesar would have crowned himself king. He was ambitious, so I killed him.

I loved Caesar, but I love Rome more.

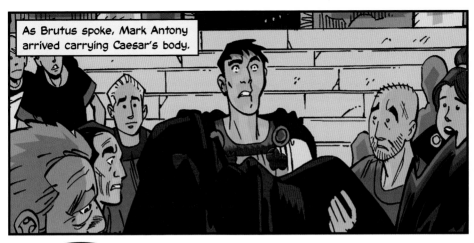

As Brutus spoke, Mark Antony arrived carrying Caesar's body.

I will use the same dagger on myself if it pleases my country.

Live, Brutus! Live!

Brutus believed he had won the people's support.

So Brutus asked the people to hear Mark Antony speak.

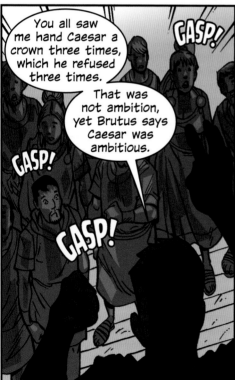

Then, Antony produced Caesar's will, which Caesar had given to him.

I must not read Caesar's will. It would anger you all too much.

Read it to us!

Read it! Read the will!

Then Antony showed the crowd Caesar's corpse.

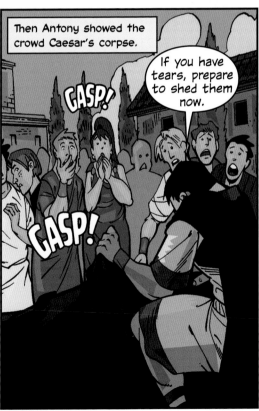

If you have tears, prepare to shed them now.

GASP!

GASP!

We all fall down when bloody treason flourishes over us.

The people carried Caesar's body as if he were truly a king.

Then they broke into riots.

All the conspirators had to flee for their lives from Rome.

And Antony had caused it all.

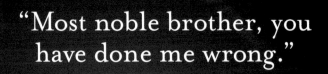

"Most noble brother, you
have done me wrong."

ACT
FOUR

The conspirators fled Rome.

They took several fast ships and sailed for Greece.

But even in another country, the conspirators knew they weren't safe.

So, they paid armies to protect them.

CLINK!

CLINK!

CLINK!

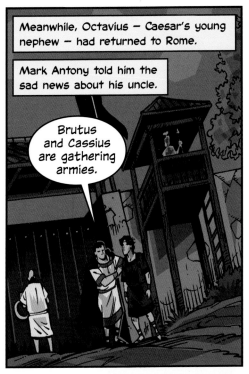

Meanwhile, Octavius — Caesar's young nephew — had returned to Rome.

Mark Antony told him the sad news about his uncle.

Brutus and Cassius are gathering armies.

Therefore let us combine our powers.

Let us do so. We are surrounded by many enemies.

And so they agreed to lead Rome's legions against the conspirators' armies.

Brutus camped his army at Sardis.

He sent a messenger named Lucilius to Cassius, who was raising his own army.

Soon, Lucilius returned with Cassius's messenger, Pindarus.

My master, Cassius, will support you, Brutus.

I do not doubt him, Pindarus.

After Cassius's messenger left . . .

How did Cassius treat you, Lucilius?

Not with friendliness.

"So call the field to rest, and let's away, to part the glories of this happy day."

ACT FIVE

The next day, Cassius and Brutus marched their armies to Philippi.

Before the battle, Brutus tried to reason with Octavius and Mark Antony . . .

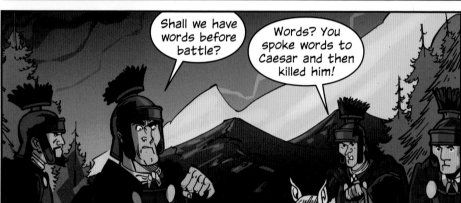

Shall we have words before battle?

Words? You spoke words to Caesar and then killed him!

I draw my sword against you, conspirators!

And I shall not put it down until Caesar's death is avenged!

I will honour you with the sharp end of my sword, Octavius.

He is unworthy of such honour.

Traitors, we defy you!

If you *dare* fight us today, meet us in the field!

Octavius and Antony left to prepare for battle against Brutus and Cassius.

I do not know if we shall meet again, Cassius.

If we do meet again, we'll be smiling.

If not, it is true this goodbye was well made.

And then the battle began.

Romans fought the soldiers Brutus and Cassius had bought.

At midday, Brutus found a weakness in Octavius's army.

He took all his men with him to attack.

While Brutus's men were distracted, Antony's men attacked Cassius's forces.

Retreat!

Cassius was forced to fall back and regroup.

Our army is surrounded by horsemen, Cassius. We have lost.

What should we do, sir?

You swore to follow my orders.

I did.

Then come here and keep your word.

Take your sword and guide the blade to my chest!

!

And so, Cassius killed himself rather than face defeat and capture.

Caesar, you are revenged with the blade that killed you.

Later that day, Brutus and his men found Cassius's body.

Oh no – Cassius!

My dear Cassius, Rome will never see your equal.

Friends, I owe more tears to this dead man than you shall see.

Let us return to the battle. We shall try our luck again in a second fight!

Angered by Cassius's death, Brutus and his army rejoined the fight.

Know me as Brutus — my country's friend!

Despite their bravery, Brutus and his men were greatly outnumbered.

CLANK!
CLANK!
CLANK!

THUD

TINK!

Eventually, Brutus's army was defeated.

CLANK!
CLANK!

TINK!

Unwilling to be captured, Brutus took some of his men to a hiding place.

There, he took them aside one by one to speak to them in whispers.

What request did Brutus ask of you?

To kill him. I refused.

What do you want from me, my lord?

Our enemies have beat us to the pit.

It is better to leap in ourselves than wait for them to push us in.

Please, hold my sword while I run into it!

I cannot!

I am your friend, sir. Please do not make me do this!

Finally, Antony and Octavius's forces drew near. All but one of Brutus's men fled in fear.

Hold up your sword!

WHOOMP!

Caesar, you can rest in peace now. I didn't kill you half as willingly as I kill myself.

Soon after, Octavius and Mark Antony found Brutus's body.

The battle, they knew, was finally over.

Brutus was the most noble Roman of them all.

All the other conspirators acted out of jealousy of Caesar, but Brutus acted honestly and for the general good.

We shall honour him with a proper funeral.

His bones will rest in my tent tonight, like an honourable soldier.

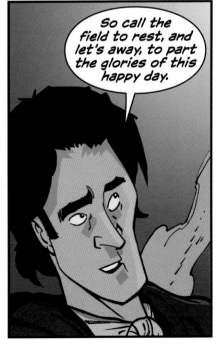

So call the field to rest, and let's away, to part the glories of this happy day.

ABOUT THE RETELLING AUTHOR

Carl Bowen is a father, husband, writer, and editor. He was born in the US state of Louisiana, lived briefly in England, and went to school in Georgia, USA, where he now lives. Carl has published a handful of novels, short stories, and comics, retelling *20,000 Leagues Under the Sea*, *The Strange Case of Dr Jekyll and Mr Hyde*, *The Jungle Book*, and "Aladdin and the Magic Lamp". He recently wrote *BMX Breakthrough*, his first original graphic novel.

ABOUT THE ILLUSTRATOR

Eduardo Garcia has illustrated for magazines in Italy, France, the United States, and Mexico. He has illustrated great characters such as Speed Racer, the Spiderman family, Kade, and many others. Eduardo is married to his beloved wife, Nancy Parrazales. They have one son, the amazing Sebastian Inaki, and an astonishing dog named Tomas.

ABOUT
WILLIAM SHAKESPEARE

William Shakespeare's true date of birth is unknown, but it is celebrated on 23 April 1564. He was born in Stratford-upon-Avon in Warwickshire and was the third of eight children to his parents, John and Mary.

At the age of 18, William married a woman named Anne Hathaway on 27 November 1582. He and Anne had three children together, including twins. After that point, Shakespeare's history is somewhat of a mystery. Not much is known about this period of his life, until 1592 when his plays first graced theatre stages in London.

From 1594 onwards, Shakespeare performed his plays with a stage company called the Lord Chamberlain's Men (later known as the King's Men). They soon became the top playing company in all of London, earning the favour of Queen Elizabeth I and King James I along the way.

Shakespeare retired in 1613, and died at the age of 52 on 23 April 1616. He was buried at Holy Trinity Church in Stratford. The epitaph on his grave curses any person who disturbs it. Translated to modern English, part of it reads:

> *Blessed be the man that spares these stones,*
> *And cursed be he who moves my bones.*

Over a period of 25 years, Shakespeare wrote more than 40 works, including poems, plays, and prose. His plays have been performed all over the world. They've also been retold in many different formats, including films, operas, TV programmes – and graphic novels like this one.

THE HISTORY BEHIND THE PLAY

The Tragedy of Julius Caesar, or *Julius Caesar,* is a fictionalized account of the rise and fall of the great Roman general. Caesar played an important role in the transition of Rome from a republic to an empire. But many Romans – including Brutus, Cassius, and Pompey – wanted Rome to remain a republic that was ruled by the people, so they assassinated Caesar.

Another of Shakespeare's Roman plays, *Antony and Cleopatra,* also features the character Mark Antony from *Julius Caesar.* Both versions of this character are based loosely on the real Mark Antony from history.

Shakespeare made up, or changed, certain historical facts in *Julius Caesar* for dramatic effect. For example: in the play, Caesar's assassination and his funeral both take place on the same day. But in reality, the death occurred on 15 March (The Ides of March) and the funeral was held on 20 March. It is likely that Shakespeare merged the two events to make the play more compact and exciting.

The title of *Julius Caesar* is misleading. While the play is a dramatization of Caesar's real life, Julius Caesar appears in only three scenes, and he is killed in the beginning of the third act. Brutus is considered to be the main character because the plot focuses on him.

Brutus is a tragic hero because, despite his good intentions and honourable nature, his shortcomings lead to his downfall.

SHAKESPEAREAN LANGUAGE

Shakespeare's writing is powerful and memorable – and sometimes difficult to understand. Many lines in his plays can be read in different ways or can have multiple meanings. Also, English spelling and pronunciation have changed over time, so the way he spelled words was not always the same as the way we spell them now. However, Shakespeare still influences the way we write and speak today. Below are some of his more famous phrases that have also become part of our language.

FAMOUS LINES FROM JULIUS CAESAR

"Beware the Ides of March." (Act I, Scene II)

SPEAKER: Soothsayer

MODERN INTERPRETATION: **Be careful on 15 March.**

EXPLANATION: In the play, a soothsayer, or psychic, warns Caesar to "Beware the Ides of March." In Caesar's time, the "Ides of March" simply meant "15 March". Caesar does not listen to the man's warning, so he dies at the hands of the conspirators on that very day. The part about the soothsayer and his prediction was likely made up by Shakespeare, although Julius Caesar was, in fact, assassinated on 15 March of the year 44 BC.

"Cowards die many times before their deaths. The valiant never taste of death but once." (Act II, Scene II)

SPEAKER: Julius Caesar

MODERN INTERPRETATION: **People who fear death suffer all their lives. People who do not fear death suffer only once – when they die.**

EXPLANATION: Shakespeare was trying to say that everyone dies eventually, so fearing death is pointless. We should accept that we cannot control when we die, and enjoy life while we're alive.

"Et tu, Bruté?" (Act III, Scene I)

SPEAKER: Julius Caesar

MODERN INTERPRETATION: **The phrase means "And you, Brutus?" in Latin.**

EXPLANATION: Caesar is surprised that Brutus, his supposed friend, is also one of the conspirators. Caesar speaks this line as Brutus stabs him, as if to say, "You have betrayed me, too, my friend?"

"Most noble brother, you have done me wrong." (Act IV, Scene II)

SPEAKER: Cassius

MODERN INTERPRETATION: **My good friend, you have wronged me.**

EXPLANATION: Cassius is accusing Brutus of disrespecting him and betraying their friendship. The two men fear that their alliance and friendship are fading, so they converse inside Brutus's tent privately to reassure each other that they are still on the same side.

"So call the field to rest, and let's away, to part the glories of this happy day." (Act V, Scene V)

SPEAKER: Octavius

MODERN INTERPRETATION: **Tell our armies to stop fighting, and let's leave. We will celebrate our victory over the conspirators.**

EXPLANATION: Octavius orders his men to stop fighting now that Brutus is dead. He then asks his army to join him in celebration of their victory.

DISCUSSION QUESTIONS

1. Do you think Cassius would have made a good ruler? What about Brutus? Why or why not?

2. Cassius and Brutus betray Caesar. Is it ever okay to betray someone? Explain.

3. Octavius and Mark Antony go to war with Brutus and Cassius. Is war ever a good thing? Discuss your answers.

WRITING PROMPTS

1. Cassius says that Rome should not be ruled by one man alone. What are the advantages of having one person make all the big decisions? What are the disadvantages? Is it better to have a group of people vote on important issues?

2. *Julius Caesar* tells the exciting story of Caesar's rise and fall. Choose an exciting part of your life and write a short, one-scene play about it. Include a cast of characters, and make sure to indicate when each character is speaking in your script.

3. Caesar's wife dreams of her husband's death. What is the scariest dream you've ever had? What is your happiest dream? Do you think dreams have hidden meanings? Write about dreams.

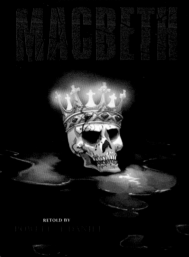

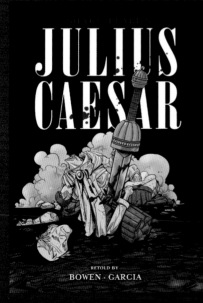

"ALL THE WORLD'S A STAGE."

— WILLIAM SHAKESPEARE